AF426108

TRESPASS

Bethany Jo Schroeder

Trespass

Collected Poems
1979–2003

With a Foreword by
Joy Ladin

Pinax Publishing
Ithaca, New York

Contents

Foreword

I met Bethany Schroeder in 1989, when I was a relatively young (late-twenties) poet who, despite sporadic efforts to find connection, community or at least networking opportunities, had been largely isolated from other poets since my graduation from Sarah Lawrence College. In one of my occasional spasms of outreach, I signed up for a poetry workshop led by Robert Haas, who had not yet become Poet Laureate of the United States. That's where I met Bethany, who had completed an MFA a few years before with great distinction at Cornell and had already published in top-tier poetry journals, including the apex predator, *Poetry*.

I didn't know that when we met, nor, as far I can recall, until I looked up her obituary while writing this foreword. She wore her CV lightly, which meant that I didn't feel the need to confess that I didn't have an MFA, and in fact had only a few publications, of the sort that do not inspire envy. Our relationship was not about credentials or careers. It was about poetry.

We spoke for a few minutes after the workshop. We had both been struck by one another's writing and critical sensibilities, i.e., neither of us had thought much of anyone else's work or comments. We also came out to one another as fellow outsiders, poets without places in the pecking orders, institutions, or movements that constituted the American poetry ecosystem at that time. That, I think, was crucial to our bond. If we had been more invested in professional connections, we probably wouldn't have connected at that workshop; we would have gravitated toward people who could help us, instead of toward the other loner at the table. In any case, we left with one another's addresses, and soon, as people did in those pre-internet decades, began exchanging letters.

Though we both lived in California and overlapped for a time in the San Francisco Bay Area, we didn't see one another much in person. Our friendship consisted of a rich poetic correspondence, several years in which we sent one another long, handwritten (at least on Bethany's part) letters filled with comments on drafts we'd exchanged, books we were reading, and occasional details about our personal lives, mostly by way of explaining delays in responding to the other's letters.

I didn't have much to say about my life outside of poetry, or at least not much that I felt I could say. For me, those were years of external stasis, of working in an office to support my and my then-wife's writing, and navigating the intestinal twists of a co-dependent marriage I couldn't talk about outside a therapist's office. But for Bethany, they were years of personal change and challenge, of raising a young daughter and, with characteristically iron-willed determination, doing what she needed to do to care for her family, putting in long hours as an emergency room, intensive care, and cardiac nurse during the AIDS epidemic and attending classes for yet another advanced degree, this time a Master of Science in Community Nursing. Bethany's work not only supported her family; it grew into an award-winning as well as life-saving career in community health and nursing that included teaching, publishing curriculum, and leading organizations that continue to make life better in the places she lived.

I didn't know much of that, and didn't really understand the glimpses her letters offered. I was years away from parenthood and an MFA, and unlike Bethany's, the work I did—administration at The State Bar of California followed by itinerant and then tenured academic teaching—left plenty of time for poetry. Perhaps because of the chasm between our circumstances, perhaps because she saw our correspondence as an opportunity to put poetry ahead of all that daily pressed upon her, Bethany didn't tell me much about her complicated personal history, her life as a parent or her work in nursing. Mostly, she wrote about poetry.

That was fine with me. Bethany's highly compressed insights and the polished phrases and elegantly terraced sentences in which she presented them helped me understand, in a way published essays could not, how to think about poetry—to think not only about individual poems and the trials of revising them but about the values and ambitions, poetic and existential, that shaped and revealed themselves through our work on those poems.

I sometimes feared I wasn't equal to the mind unfurling through Bethany's closely but neatly written pages. I worried that she could see through me, that beside her tough-minded critical sophistication, my ideas about poetry seemed like a metaphor-soaked muddle. Those anxieties forced me to think more clearly, to try to grow into (or at least sound like) a poet and correspondent Bethany would admire the way I admired her. Among many other benefits, Bethany's letters punctured the bubble of self-regard in which I had protected and isolated myself as a poet. More than that: in ways I was not at all aware of at the time, Bethany readied me to leave that bubble. It is no coincidence that during our correspondence I began to apply to MFA programs, and was finally accepted into one. Ironically, that acceptance and my subsequent relocation to the East Coast led, on my side at least, to the lapsing of our letter exchanges, but thanks to Bethany's example and intellectual companionship, I arrived in academia well-practiced in analytical literary and critical discourse.

The same year, 1992, that I entered my MFA program, Bethany completed her Master of Science degree. As this long-delayed first book, a selection of almost a quarter century of writing from 1979 through 2003, shows, Bethany continued writing poetry long after we lost touch, but much of her time, creativity and writing were devoted to her work as a nurse and community health activist. Bethany didn't think much of poetry rushed into the world, but had her circumstances been different, her talent, seriousness, and the brilliant start to her career would, I am sure, have meant that her first collection would have appeared decades ago and been one of many.

Poetry programs, workshops, craft lectures, and writers conferences often feature references to the dangers of letting life interfere with writing poetry, one of the least-remunerative of American artistic endeavors. These dangers tend to be particularly great for women, who are generally expected and socialized to put others' needs before their own creativity, and even greater for mothers and those who feel called to not only write about the world but to make it a healthier, more caring place.

Bethany, obviously, was in the extremely high risk category. She loved poetry deeply, but she loved people more. American poetry is the poorer for the hard choices she made between her loves, but as a country, America is better for them.

And though it limited the time she had for poetry, Bethany's love for people inspired many of her poems, including nuanced portraits like "In the Berry Patch," which says of an aunt named Sharon, who the poem sardonically refers to as "my uncle's mistake,"

>   ….Sometimes
> she'd wander past the row
> we tended, and looking out,
> set flush her bosom
> against the fence. She'd say,
> "Impress me in a good wife's wind."
> I didn't understand her then.
> I wonder now what grace or compensation
> bound us groundward together—
> pips inside a seed pod: separate,
> and so much the same...

Love also lights her exquisite descriptions of landscapes, animals, and especially birds, such as the intimately playful "Geese," which opens

> I've never heard such gossip.
> You fly over the house
> in family coteries—
> your calls to one another
> rasping and full as this blast
> of silence you leave behind.
> How could I know
> you'd complain about front winds
> and tail winds and rest stops
> between landing strips?

You can't read these poems, or any in the book, without being struck by Bethany's delight in and devotion to language, often expressed through obscure but oddly perfect words mined from her wide-ranging, deep-delving vocabulary and deployed with startling precision. Though as committed as any poet of our generation to vernacularity, Bethany didn't shy away from literary-sounding language; she gloried in it. The resulting poems have both the smack and urgency, the gestural physicality, of spoken utterances, and an old-fashioned opulence of music and diction that lends a grave glamour to the most mundane of subjects, like those geese with their "family coteries" and the "grace or compensation" that, when walking among crops with aunt Sharon, "bound us groundward together." In other hands, phrases like these might seem precious or overwrought; in Bethany's, the gorgeousness of the language expresses her intertwined passions for language, life and the world, and the intensity with which she gave her heart and mind to them.

Heart and mind: line after line both brims with restrained emotion and gleams with the active intelligence working through it, a form of intelligence in which thinking is fused to imagination. Bethany's mind is manifest not only in lapidary phrases such as "the new year's poulticed verb" ("A Winter Breviary") but in the folding and unfolding of her complicated, highly enjambed sentences. The tension between the meaning that freights each line and that of the larger statements to which those lines contribute can be so great that her sentences feel like labyrinthine high-wire acts, series of sure-footed twists, shifts, and leaps held aloft by the steely thread of her syntax.

This "strong syntax," as Donald Davie would have called it, not only forces us to think our way through Bethany's poems; it enacts, embodies in language, the mind that animates those poems, giving us the sense we are thinking with her, through her, sharing her depth of reflection on scenes and relationships that, for the most part, the poems only partially permit us to know.

That combination of intimacy and privacy, of revelation and concealment, was characteristic of our correspondence too. Her letters, like her poems, always reminded me how much more there was to know about Bethany's life and thought. Even Bethany's capacious vocabulary and intricate syntax could never hold or communicate more than a fraction of her mind, her soul, her life.

I've lost her letters, in the course of many moves, but here are her poems, reminding me, as she always did, of how much more there is to learn, to love, to write. As she writes of aunt Sharon :

> I didn't understand her then.
> I wonder now what grace or compensation
> bound us groundward together—
> pips inside a seed pod: separate,
> and so much the same...

And so much the same.

Joy Ladin

xv

I. Lamplit Tents (1979–1983)

Instincts

Is the black cat
in our basement feral or
are her instincts
sharper than ours?
You say she won't live
with us: she'll eat
the food I bring
so long as I
don't touch her.

I see her eyes beam
back gold against
my flashlight.
I think my own
eyes must lose their color
under the floorboards
where she waits
to see I am
what I offer.

On the Venice Beach

The little girl on the plane
Who turned her doll's head around
To look at me.
— J. D. Salinger

The girl sits sideways,
her arm extended
along the dashboard
of the car. She chews
at her lower lip
until it opens
while her young mother
drives too fast between
the traffic signals.
Glancing off her cheek,
sunlight hits the pearl
in the girl's earring
as if it is important that they meet
through the windshield glass.
Still she doesn't see
what the old women
on the Venice beach
discover: driftwood
banked by the night tide
for morning's pleasure;
small shells whose colors
liven with water and sand.

Huckster

for Archie Ammons

Who could upset the bark
bullied from the depth of his chest
at an awful rate, but clear
as the sound boot heels
make in hard dirt?
Hearing the same lines each
turn of the fair we see him
dustier, but no less fierce
for the sun's perfect set
on his full height the hawk of
syllables pulls up.
When dark hustles the last stragglers
off grounds he, rounding
torso to knees,
squats down to massage
the loops of his hucklebones.
He started like this—
hunkering hips on a sackcloth
stretch of market, peddling
to passersby from a basket in which
his horse might tow
bargains or the warm air home.
Then huckster, hawker, peddler
barked the dreams
from others' brittle tongues.
No beast to help him now:
he has community . . .
the camp whores, geeks, and animals,
lamplit tents where men wash down
the noises of trade.

Rhythms

Karl says we flatter ourselves
in trying to save a life. He hates
the confusion of hands on unfamiliar flesh,
the clatter of stainless steel and plastic
pushed to an excess of excellence.
He hates the blood on his smock
got there by our vain resistance
to some stranger's death.
He wants the green walls to be quiet,
the mayo stands lined up
beside empty beds, the surgical lights
kept off in response to a vision
that lets life proceed how it will.
He wants the careful truck
of cell to cell to state such harmonies
as angels know.

         When he puts
his hands on men
who can no longer put
their hands on him, he says he hates
our overrated reliance on skill.
We should dismiss the grief
in love grown too completely physical
when hearts refuse their difficult rhythms
and lungs will not fill,
will not consent to a relationship
with air. He calls our care
indulgence and thinks we'd do better
to make less noise about the life
we won't let go gracefully back to God.

A Winter Breviary

Mute dreams bow down to the listener now.
The dogs crowd snaggled planks
around the house and whimper
at a cold-blown moon.
Two jays claim their early feed
below the hen-shed eaves. Rain
stampedes the sick-room glass.

My broken bones rehearse some simple mendings.
Cells tuck and roll the fractured space
like winter bending
into spring: the ashes green
their weathered stems; woods
snap like white-winged sheets
across the open air.

Nature chafes inside this winter wrap.
The dogs quiet down as the moon
battens her hatch. Blue jays grouse
about stray eggs then eat
their fill. The window
sloughs its skin and sounds
the new year's poulticed verb.

Butter and Guns

(1982)

Khrushchev rolls his eyes
under a wrinkled pate.
He's stuck in his western suit,
looking the part of someone
a kid can recognize.

He's sick of history,
over-worked, his nailbeds
soft and ashen:
here's Khrushchev standing
with comrades at the Kremlin Wall.
I was twelve.
I can remember
him telling the world
it mattered who ruled
the Russian state.

Now Khruschev puts pennies
on Brezhnev's eyes.
Like a grandame
pruning violets, he fusses
over the dead man's tie,
seems to stop in some emotion,
sighs and sighs,
and wags his head
at the khaki-breasted soldiers
guarding the casket ends.

8

Does he wonder if any of them,
his comrades or him,
were ever so young?—
perfectly smooth as a nimbus,
hollow and clear.

Imaginary Gardens

. . . a dream you can touch is a myth.
— Carlos Fuentes

for Michael Schroeder

I too am curious.
I want to see its haunches heave
across horizons primed for the movements
of unicorns. I want the myth
grown out of dreams when we say
what we mean and say
"now this," "touch this."
I wonder at the horn Pliny wrote
is an antidote for poison.
And while some might confuse it
with the sable antelope,
like you, I've called in the night
and sometimes
it has answered me.

The Swiss Inn

for Harry Lawton

It's an old house
with modern makeshifts
at the back
strung round
by barb and wire
like a tidy German camp.
The tenants pen their dreams
in the air with echoes,
pieces of found memory.
This one wants his mother,
broom-woman whose swift kick
he knows now to prefer
to the slow fall down
of Valium. That one paces,
paces on the lawn, forging
his escape like a signature,
but free he hurries long strides home
to the Swiss Inn.

There's no use
trying to hide them—
better to fence them in,
count heads between shifts
of street-dressed nurses.
The tenants mime their keepers
when they're handed cups
of colored pills.

Then the sane retreat
as evening warms
to the door, to the sensible
shelf and shell of House.
Seeing the nurses leave
is the only way to know
who's who, until
the tenants prime
the night, broadcasting
their chorus again.

Tug-of-War

Woodcutters' Fair, 1982
Trumansburg, New York

They match the teams by weight.
Men and a handful of women
line up at the rope.
Waverly wrestles Cayuga Hose,
but the Zimmermans win
the war—a family whose six
veterans know how to tug through
the worst of New York's snow.
When ages 0–10 tug rope,
they copy their elders' pull,
banding on either end
of the bright flag hung
just above the ground.
"Dig in!" the grownups yell.
Children wave and muster
strength with calls from
the crowd—holler and clap,
no matter which side wins.
Arcadia manned by imps;
parents hurdle stands and fence
for hugs at the winners' ground:
T'burg Fire ribbons each kid.
Baseball caps flash the names
of neighboring factions,
urge Culver Lanes or The Spot
on us. We shuffle here

and there. The MC says, "If you
hadna came, we wouldna all
been together,"
as day tugs night
across our heads and shoulders
and we wind
our precarious conference home.

rock

a friend brought me this black rock
we were never lovers although we
worried the possibility to death
he said he'd be King Auk
if i'd be mistress sloe-eye
and ready at the spot of our nursery
male penguins give treasure
to their future mates
he wanted me to have this one

now you bring the rock to bed for luck
we let it mean our pin-wings
itch to start a rookery where we
might birth such pieces of present and past
as this smooth basalt has

Flinch

for Cory Brown

The purple finch woos missus finch
under the cherry tree: they've come
to gather seed. One thrill,
another thrill until she pecks
him back to where he sits, his berry-
tinctured head and beak set
straight and stunned and still.

Ambitious bird, you'll get
no joy from her whose
nest you've strawed, whose nest
she's filled and that you both
must feed, though wings in the air
your voice will carry
and tell the world the matter.

They Look Like Yellow Flies

for Cory Brown

coralled around the cardinals'
paired "what cheer" "what cheer,"
the black-capped chickadees
tining plethoric threats at screwbirds
scooting down the ash where
hairy peckers eat suet
in iron wired on the tree
the plug-ugly jays crow for:
"queedle" "queedle" "caw"
back at hawks hawking the same
way above the thrasher
bumping leaf root, while the gold
finches wait-see-sit, then flap in dread-of
what can't be got to by clamor.

Geese

for Ken McClane

I've never heard such gossip.
You fly over the house
in family coteries—
your calls to one another
rasping and full as this blast
of silence you leave behind.
How could I know
you'd complain about front winds
and tail winds and rest stops
between landing strips?

North Carolina says New York's
baited its geese. The hunters
call you theirs and swear about your
absence as you bitch
across the greeny wake of fall,
the unpredictable northern fall.
Your goose beaks dibble and hoe
through the air, routing out
pockets of seed corn
unseeded yet.

The earth is a hunt and peck of color.
Winds rock leaves off trees.
The cold nights brown and crisp
the brightest ones, leaving a litter
of yellow spiced with occasional red.

My beautiful reds! Blown out
over summer's horizon
where geese braze in the glow,
dropping their feathers,
their bills on the ground.

Weegee

American News Photographer,
1900-1968

You took pictures
of murder victims, murderers,
whores cuffed at the ankles—
strapped to one another.
Your biographers wrote that you slept
in a bug heap across
from the station, jimmied
your scanner on its frequency,
left when the squad cars did.
You thought lookers-on
telling as the scene,
shot women and school kids
eager to watch.

      New York
 in the 40s was gruesome.
 I want to shake your bones
out of the grave—
the city's the same;
the country's the same;
some still play
mysterious stakes, Ouija.
The planchette writes
its automatic hand while
I sift a confluence of
shards and festering scabs you
scratched off the inner city.

II. Blackberry Winter (1984–1988)

Women's Work

Thirty years after you made her
I washed the Raggedy Ann.
I'm a formalist, too. I like
the boundaries out where I can see them,
but not so far they can't be reached.

I washed her clothes. I pressed
her hand-laced petticoats and, I
confess, I let my fingers wait
on the dotted dress where
you had sewn a row of phlox.

I imagine Grandpa smiled, called it
women's work as he watched you
net and whip through the afternoon.
He approved each stitch, knew blues
you chose by the color of his eyes—

he left me that: the expectation
of someone knowing my work
as it matters, while you
showed me how to do it,
how to get it fixed.

In the Berry Patch

Before I knew women were other than
curlers and cakes I knew Sharon,
my uncle's mistake, the aunt
of my farming summers.
We'd meet in a field of timothy,
her hair still blonde, her eyes
blue as the lupine we picked
going back to her house and the bull
of our talk and the berries
we'd weeded of quackgrass.

From her I learned that Sharon means
plain like a section of earth
one could travel or farm. Sometimes
she'd wander past the row
we tended, and looking out,
set flush her bosom
against the fence. She'd say,
"Impress me in a good wife's wind."
I didn't understand her then.
I wonder now what grace or compensation
bound us groundward together—
pips inside a seed pod: separate,
and so much the same.

Some of us blamed her for leaving.
Some of us still hold a grudge.
I remember instead her, arch-backed,

butt-up, over the berry plants.
She almost always
thought we should go
in the other direction,
away from the fields and the house.

Forked Tale

The swallow forces
her nest fast as a root
on Aunt Faye's kitchen window ledge.
Straw sticks through
the frame she won't clean
up after. Let the tiny fibers flag

from their stems, let
traces of her husband's fields
dust faucets and porcelain, let her
sewing wait. Aunt Faye's
learning joy, the swallow's clinical
grace, as she leans into the cross and promise

of her sink remembering
how her mother's lips unpinched
when the first swallow flew summer in.

Yarn

For fifty winters
Minnie rubbed the ewes' hard
undersides while afterbirth
splattered her chaps and lambing boots.

In spring she docked the yearlings in,
pinned ears or branded rumps
with the farm's tattoo yelling "git"
when mothering sheep circled the fence.

Twice each summer week
she hauled up sugar, coffee, chew
to the Basques whose collies
yipped, tucked tails, and hid

behind the sheepcamp wheels. Through fall
she helped the hired hands shear sheep,
dip sheep, and mend the sheepcote's
splintering tines and slats.

When Sam retired she said
"now there's an end to sheep,"
purling the warp and weft
in sweaters and scarves her family keeps.

Sudden Weather

Minnie sat on the down-filled bed
pulling the combs through her henna hair,
and Sam could refuse her nothing.
Which bolt of cloth did she want
or cut-glass lamp did she long
to mend by the light of?
Her chickens could spackle their coop,
her bum-lambs skitter and twist
in her bum-lamb pen,
her milk cows stand forgotten.
Until they met he never thought
of making beauty his.

              The children
came in pairs of tow-heads and red-heads
and the farm couldn't wait. Minnie's
bright hair paled as Sam stacked hay
against sudden weather, his hips hanging
loose over late summer grain.
She wanted something then—
that he resist the fields, take up
her loveliness again, his hands and face
sewing knots in her hair.

Desire and fear snigger
like twins in a double-take
of mistaken identity.
Still Minnie wanted something then:
she drew instead the farm's hard sell

and Sam's fool ignorance of her wish.
As they aged, neither switch
nor frizzet wig recalled in him
the hair that held a lover's scent.
She set their wedding portrait
on the mantel's lip where
nothing changed or came untrue or
was ever spent.

Spooner's Cove

At Montana d'Oro

Lathering swells suggest the calamities
bones return to tell of.
The headlands look mean and seductive.
The ocean curbs eyefuls of its
luster on the shore.
Barnacles truss the seaside hull
of poppy-covered bluffs, and spindrift
slips a caul over us and the rocks
the gulls settle on.

We think some secret's in the cove
the law protects or protects us from.
That earth's indifferent here,
that pleasure's rough as the musseled shoal
we hold between our toes.
Still in spring we straddle the land
our government fences off,
join the limpets clinging to broad sea arms
gone stiff against each roller's sudden weight,

and pick the plovers' slurred
"whe-re-ee" out of the tide's white noise.
We laugh, dismissing what we miss
from our romance—
the houses on the quay, the quay,
an oarsman guiding his yawl
from ship to harbor. Nothing
conscious stays in Spooner's Cove:
the cold and urgent ocean is,
and flowers are gold when saying makes them so.

Home

In Memory, Sharon McPhee

The road commissioner's men hold back
a multitude of springs in borrow ponds along
the roadside. Each manbuilt
water-womb's a bucket
of startled breeders
disclosing its turn at
gain or decay when I come by
the brim. Cowslips border some
ponds and flatter the bee.
Willows withe their hair
in their hair on others, while
some ponds cradle the muck of
stickleback, pike, and nettle-
bush where lovers
crawl under to bake
on the steamy loam.
Yet I have searched the ponds
near home, watched waterbugs
cleave to water leaving
no sign of their passing,
of plain-brute industry,
no scar. I've seen
backswimmers kicking up
pondbloom that blooms
the same again for
kingfishers diving for fish.

And I've strayed fresh gravel
across Lee County roads and then,
with cheatgrass shunting its wicks
in my socks and pants,
I have looked back at nothing changed
and walked on home.
Someday I might find a borrow pond
gone, evolved in its own destruction
to fen or farmland, though
everywhere I see water and wings stirring
time's midden, man's landfill.

Buffalo

The water tank sags between
posts dug in the Carolina clay.
Its red metal shell upbraids function:
trash gathers in the fault
its red ends hinge
like a red kiss to winds
that last night squalled
limbs, cones, straw
from the southern pines.
I sink weight-pooling
prints in the ice grass
through clod under the broken
tank my tar-heel friends call Buffalo.
And "Buffalo" marked in white
spray paint and a Palmer's hand
reads the tank,
meaning what?
Meaning useless now?
That the earth's drift-up-and-pull
and famous weather deceived
in ways men try to reconcile.
Or meaning just used up
as the tank's outside
will be when lovers write
Jenny + Rick and
Forever Marianne and
Jo Loves Jon in '84—
the qualifications
grim and peculiar
among all that buffalo.

Blackberry Winter

Through winter's laying in and every
early camphored night
we asked what color eyes
would our eyes make—
how much would the brain weigh—
would blood and blood in us
determine flesh and blood.
I read the almanac for signs;
you threw the *I Ching*
and ordered a parents' guide.

Now something resists.
Cattails grow like pickets
along the swamp; privets
border the wood and lawn.
You leave our house for projects
spring discovers:
I scrub at the shut-in walls,
store mufflers and gloves against
next winter's cold.
We live as the farmers live—
one day and then another;
one season humbling the last.

But does the sky behave?
Can the rain hold back? Can the grass?
When you've settled the dust
at your bench, when I've needled
our wool into drawers, we could

go down by the blackberry copse
where vetch holds cover over
the coming fruit. There
I could make love to you
the way the last
cold snap of winter
touches ground. The farmwives
call such weather luck—
they say berries will spill
from their metal pails
in a rush of flowers,
white and promising
colors of plums.

Ironwood

Cole calls the ironwood a guest.
Brought to the desert fifty years ago,
it thrives now under the pink light.
"Not like a smoketree," dying at every
wrong altitude, folding in wind.

Our eastern ironwoods are sturdy, too,
local and plentiful. We like
their muscular skins, bud-browned after winter.
Once I tried to carve our names on one
behind the pigpen saying *shit shit*
as my knife flaked at tree cells. Insignificant.
What fool tries to write on ironwood?
And failing that, who dreams
the *A* and *A* of lovers on a tree?

You want the truth? When I saw
Cole's ironwood I dreamed you
and a forest of tough and heavy trees.
I dreamed the whitetail browsing there and
how I laughed to hear how
ironwood rots when touching ground.
I dreamed a tree and both of us admiring it.

Nutshell

Able to dupe the cuckoo's
song and trumpet spring
and be the intimates
of men, sparrows can't stop
the cowbird slipping
her egg into their
nest before she
rides off
on the backs of
great slow cattle.
A parasite
eating parasites,
the cowbird abandons her young
for the ride.
I've heard
how sparrows
will stuff their foster
baby's tireless
gimme, gimme
with flowers and grubs,
his witless body extending
the shadow around them.
And I've wondered if I'd put up
as much to get as much.

Hound

Up again. The sun was always up
in southern California as I
slipped from under the sheets,
not wanting to roil
the jetsam of our double berth.

On the street, our neighbor's
dachshund scuffed and tottered home.
The morning's urine wet
his feet, then he heaved on,
eyes wide with long-eared standing.

I thought, I'd swap sailor's bunk
for hound house to see him
skip instead of scrape the walk.
Beast, broken at the back
from gutter shots, from trenchant air
reminds me of us, of the hole
in the bed our bodies make
when we grope at the space
left by our pegless legs. By sunrise
we tried over and failed to jump.

Me and the Heron

for Bob Bosak

Watching him
watch for the possibility
of fish, eyes scrupulous and farouche, his great
gray egg of a body stumped over the pond,
I know the difference between us.
Once satisfied, he'll paddle
into the sky, celebrating the bank, his
prey, his vigorous carcass as he dumps
his own sweet stink behind him.
And I will be too old for most things
before the natural passing
of my own merciless witness
frees me from being
bothered by shit.

Natural Selection

Across the backlot's crab and devilgrass
past jimson corrupting the footpath
in the burnt-out shed's half-light
I watched you wiping soot from what
the fire and rats had left behind.

And thought how the happy
survive and multiply and, getting
others, usually forget first wishes.
But what did you wish in saving
your mother's letters—her rains

of worry and worship sent
to dorm addresses in the 60s?
Or your guitar, its long fretted neck
bubbled under the ash, your porkpie cap
formerly pert and workable?

These, and political buttons, their
fairings heat-bent and brittle as sin,
and a political banner I almost heard flap in
the air again, and gears from the press
you oiled and cursed and loved

into radical print. "Just stuff,"
you said, shrugging it off
like a bruise, like a soft spot
gone hard, reproving what was

implacable and raw in you,
what made your human privilege
literal from the start, what made
you, dreamer-you, lay away in our shed
the parts of your sometimes
high and sometimes ordinary life.

Sortie

for Bob Morgan

Dusk, and the streetlamps snap
in blue accord across the park. From my bench
by the owl pen I watch the lovers leave,
the last of the families leave,
packing their good opinions home.

Moles scratch out of their burrows
and crickets chirr under the trees. The owl
listens for sport the moon orders, clucks
eagerly, spreading her wings as though
no cage could secure the park from her habits.

And when she whoops from her gallery
roost or heckles the rails of her keep, she is
night's advocate, needy and grieved
for what she sees and I still half believe
of the darkness, teasing life.

As I quit her level stare, I think
of home and the troubles there that favor dull
and comforting dreams, and I want to wake
tonight to the sough of her tremolo,
the salvo of her wingbeats.

III. MONKEY (1989–1994)

Trespass

We stop where the Pierce and Stanley
families rest, their plots secured by
dry wild grasses and bone-white clamshells
cupping the tops of graves
as our hands could.
Behind us I hear the Atlantic
whose winds surprised these
inland miles with sand,
surprise them still.
The sand drifts west, grazing
cemetery crosses and head-
stones as it passes.

Does wanting proof
of what passes draw us in
to visit the dead we never knew?
A stand of bald cypresses
hems the farthest graves to the road
where you stand, camera ready
to shut on an image
twinned in your lens.
Row after row of markers
and I see you
upright like them—
dumb mark of a man.

The lilies spin
in their plastic cups.
Let offerings turn or stay:
no one will know if we
lie down between graves,
face east with the dead,
our bodies making a nidus
of bones in the sand.
I compare our births and names
and those of the dead, touch wet fingers
to wind, thinking
my trespass against you.

Circle

I. Our Mothers

Nothing favors the day.
Patients held under the sheets
by their fugitive rhythms—
most of them

past ambition—
curtains half drawn,
observation lamps left
off or skillfully dimmed.

The women smelling
of soap and chloroform.
One says how feeble her
mother is—latching

the doors on fantastic hazards,
repeatedly patting
the cold stove—patrolling
the cellar stairs

for steps or the trigger
of uninvited light.
One asks
what any of us are

when our mothers break
our hearts—as if
that were the issue.

The others look down,
images brimming—
flat hands
in their laps softening
like the circle of sick around them.

II. Dream

You hate miracles but you enter
this one, willing to be deceived.

The frame houses—their clapboards
glinting like glass, uniform pickets trim,

the junipers marking the way to porches
and street-side passages in.

Your caught breath sears—the morning air
uncertain as your quivering lip.

You say "mother" when you see her,
"mother" as if she were there

wrapped in green gingham, sweeping the walk
along the road you dreamed you wanted.

"Mother," "mother," although she won't answer,
although her hair's the absent color of her skin,

although the only shadow under the sun is yours
looking back at the range of her doing

when she ushered you past a collection
of stones on the wrong path home.

III. The Natural

When I saw her I brightened
wondering what
if she weren't mine
would I love her
say love again
would I love her
could I still
imagine her head
pushed free
then breathing
as I took my breath
all the cells of me
pumped up
in the expectation
she'd be the vowel
the open note
the song sung
in my own idiom.

Mayapples

Twelve days overdue, I walk
with you to hold on, to forget.
Every bush bears the sudden eye,
the once over, then over again with patience.
All spring I've watched
these fields become new meadows,
although we say they want water.
Now the asters open early and the flies
have been no bother. Where we stop on the path
we foresee dry panicles of oats
burnt brown by June,
altogether gone by August.

Decadence has its own high style.
Between clumps of burdock and bluets
we find mayapples,
frail as debutantes,
each blossom borne in the crotch
of two lobed leaves, protective palms
swung over the heads of flowers, whose petals
hang in swags of cells cinched stiff
at the stalk. Skin to skin,
my fingers curl to their touch.

I kneel too deep to the ground and
reach for you to help me up. Near as we are
there is the distance of one to come
between us. In your pull

and my push up I think I see her,
two weeks late and swathed
in her own shucked flesh.
Just May, and already turning to dust.

Warning

In Memory, Pam Licata

I see your petal-colored arm
above the latex gloves you wore,
breasts straining your lapel,
your eyes obedient to fear,
your savage cheeks and shoulders straight,
your strawberry hair.

I see the desert's late-in-the-day pink light
we said we loved, ever changing light,
too close to other changes—
the provocations
of fame, of paradise, the amorous
rose on the lips of exile.

Covenant

Safety doors shut hard
on the desert heat outside of
the hospital ward where her husband
waits, telling a dream to the white wings of his sheets.
As suddenly as they meet
he is himself again,
no longer the ashen traveler lately withdrawn
from the dead, but a man whose arms
receive her arms and the small of her spine
and the richly wired bulb of her head.

Each of them speaks, recasting
the bones of half a century. Her hands
stroke his. His eyes welcome hers, two lovers
snared under droning fluorescent lights.
He whispers how like the animals he has become,
unable to plan, helpless
to say where he will go.
And then he's gone.
Slung like sticks upon the bed,
she holds him close as if to hold their living in.

Before she stands she settles
the crease of his lids, kisses
his stiffening lips, and rethinks eternity.
The shape of it shifts from what they've said
would be release
to months or years or worse

confined to memory. That the ordinary
will get too big: his unlit pipe, food he liked,
books half-read and cracked at the back.
His arms forever opened wide.

What Remains

. . . the deathless
  nobility
   at the core of all ordinary things
      —Gary Snyder

He wakes
wound up
by his unwinding
clock, blinks
back the sleep
of mortal extremis,
drawn downstairs
to coffee and vitamins,
each restorative confounding
the work of the other.

She knows his habits:
first to read,
to think, to make
a pretense
at leisure,
then to shower, to groom
away the remains of
yesterday's pleasures, an hour
to simulate some
manly order.

And knowing this
she knows the instant

to enter their room,
what to do, where
to stand to watch his
plain raw flesh,
the slope of his neck,
one slim leg bent, one
flexed to accept the studied
press of his pants.

Woman Naming

She shuts up her heart
when she cooks.
Under the armor
of hunger she can
ignore distractions:
his voice at the door;
no voice at the door;
the neighborhood talk
when she brushed
her hand on her lips
and brought his kisses
to her mouth again. The thought

of her own company
most days, most nights.
How this is some
kind of hell to live
like her mother,
her mother's mother
in catalogues of things
feared—just the suggestion
of having once lived.
How she mothers
the blades of bussed
kitchen knives.

In Difference

There is unity
where space reveals
its material
edges where land
and water assemble
separate where
waking we praise
the other one
dreaming *me*
not *you*.

Monkey

Tonight he wraps
    his legs around her
        back and strokes

the furrow between her breasts
    and rubs her belly's
        thickening lip,

and the wind
    in his voice stirs
        her fallen expectations

as he says again how
    he won her once and wants her
        still as much, or more, no, more.

Is she surprised
    at the unlikeliness of love,
        the man huddled up

in his addled bliss,
    the enigma of his fragile breath
        pulled into the steady

mix of hers, their
    fear perplexed by wild
        and deft fulfillments?

That development starts
    at the top, works down
        resisting flight,

the aboriginal hiss
    of early light and
        harassed dusk, the impulse

shot through to his
    splendid eyes when she reaches
        for his tail.

Making Love

When I ask
what you're thinking
you say the several names
of God and that mine
is one of them.

IV. To Heart (1994–2003)

Let Me Wash Your Feet

Let me wash your feet.
Let me press them dry
in the faded cotton folds
of my skirts.

Let me fill my house
with your house—my heart
with yours—my eyes with
what you see.

Let me wake in the night
to the wild guide
your sleep petitions.
Let the bend

of my back
respond to yours,
my hands complete themselves
in yours, my words

prefigure yours
when you're asked
If you live alone,
whose feet will you wash?

You Are My Father

Now that we ourselves are older,
having started to morph
from the hint of a slope
to something shell-like,
a little pale, a little delicate,

I can think without cringing
of the only time I saw
my father's bare chest.
He had pulled off what clothes
he could, his shoes

and jacket and shirt, his belt,
perhaps, and jumped into the foamy water
after me in a dinghy bobbing across the bay.
March on Santa Catalina.
I was 12 and suddenly quiet to see

the half-naked form of my father stripped
then launched over the waves,
his white arms pulling him
toward the vessel, his outline
vague and brave and pathetic.

He was no more the source or repository
of unconditional love,
Although I did still love him then,
despite knowing he had made himself unlovable.
And knowing, too, that one day

not far in the future I'd step
up to my place with you,
where for a moment I'd consider arrogance
but choose instead the truth, the absolute:
Now you are my father. Save me.

Dubiety

shares with satiety
a moment when the lights go on
and a surfeit of possibilities
present themselves:
She loves me and I am
the most complete of persons
or she loves me not
and I am a dead man, dead
after failed and dangerous
and over-ambitious hope.

What fed my faith,
looking out over the green field
at all of the stars, afraid
I might never find you,
determined I would?
Hope that called out
loneliness and the rages of wanting you.
Hope I repulsed then suffered
to intone, "I loved you.
I love you still, dubiety."

Sufficient

From the beginning you see
your focus commandeered
by his banter about anxiety and money
and the fools they are for not loving you.
You are diverted
from yourself for so long
in the end
you're the partner of a sum,
the two of you, a pair.

On the other hand you're not alone,
no small consolation
in a time following the millennium—
only a moment into the future—
when he either will or won't be a success,
not quite, but almost
self-absorbed, either way
assured of status each of you
will come to collect.

Induced

As in the beginning and end of your life
together; your introductory
love—the baptism
that left you scared,
still leaves you scared
one or the other won't stay.

As in an excuse that closes
on a convincing rift,
the preamble of goodbye.

As in knowing how what you do
makes the other one feel awful.

Then back to the start as in, of course,
how you met; smoke
in a crowded room,
the smell of dust in the air,
no motive beyond your initial contact
and how almost at once
you had to turn back from desire
for the various stars that accompanied
that still-bright but vanishing sun.

Her Daughter

She put her nose to the bedding
close enough to smell the two of them
as she quickly lifted the sheets from the quilts,
rustling out the possibilities.

Where had she first caught them?
Kissing on a swatch of burnt lawn or
was it at the outer edge of the garage
where she watched him press her daughter

into the space between a closed door
and the building's southwest corner?
For the first time ever she could see
his abandon, and as for her daughter?

Her daughter had coiled along his length,
then spread out over him like a pale, cooling star.

To Heart

for J.B.

Not only the organ,
its shape, its function,
not only the open, global middle,
the pulsing, fractious region,

but also to heart,
encourage, to animate,
to give heart to, to take
to heart, to fill up

one centrality from an-
other, to heart it with one's space,
to concentrate, consolidate
the halves into a heart.

Strength

Countries, muscular
in their arrogant and terrible pride,
with *regimes* instead of governments,
impregnable, unrelenting,
exactly not what we had called for
when at first we considered strength,
the gun's mightiness,
the frailty of words.

Nor like the potency and force,
the mainstay of our attachment—
and a firm support it seemed—
as we clung,
one tremulous wretch to another,
tricked into thinking—anything!
Then shamed in our cross recriminations
that we'd gone impossibly, irredeemably wrong.

Oh, lover, who does not know strength
when he sees it? If he runs afoul of it,
how fast does he run?
Fleeter than ever before
he leaps over
stones and fences and bushes,
a fearless man,
based on all the reports of the day.

Dear Husband

I read that the three stages of faith
are receipt, assent, and surrender,
which must be true, for I happily enter
these stages and am succumbed
by them every day with you. For years
I moved between them, but now I live
in their energy, for their energy,
inhaling and exhaling their syllables
as the representation of this state of faith.
Because of you, the curriculum.

Because of you one duty just because
I want to. Reverence—
not in obedient response but
for the sake of something shared, good guy
that you are stumping up the step
to meet me after a day somewhere
in the world, faithful to me, altogether
too abstract until you pull me to you
at the top of our porch, lips to lips,
face to face in faith.

Bethany Schroeder was born in Pocatello, Idaho, on June 12, 1952. Her father, Richard Schroeder, taught in private schools and later served in several as headmaster. Bethany grew up in various parts of the country as her family (including her mother, Sharon, and younger brothers George and Michael) moved to take advantage of her father's career opportunities, finally completing high school at Woodmere Academy on Long Island. Every summer was spent at the sheep and cattle ranch in Idaho owned by her maternal grandparents, an experience that gave her a lasting appreciation for country ways and country people and provided a source of material for much of her later poetry.

Schroeder and her first husband, Andrew Douglas, moved west, eventually settling in Santa Barbara, California, where she worked for three years as a florist's apprentice. Determined to secure a living that she could depend on, Schroeder took an associate degree in nursing at the College of the Desert and then enrolled as an English major at the University of California at Riverside to prepare for a career as a writer, escaping during this period from a brief and abusive second marriage. It was in Riverside that she met and married her third husband, Jon Bosak, with whom she remained until her death.

Schroeder graduated from UCR in 1981 with high honors, including Phi Beta Kappa, Deans' National Honor List, UCR Outstanding Woman Student of the Year, and the Ina Coolbrith Memorial Poetry prize, the highest California award for undergraduate poetry. She supported herself at this time working nights as head of nursing in charge of the emergency room at Riverside County General Hospital, which served as the trauma center for an area of over 7000 square miles.

In 1982 her poetry gained her a Sage Fellowship to Cornell, where she studied with poets Kenneth McClane, Phyllis Janowitz, Robert Morgan, and A. R. Ammons. This period was artistically and academically rewarding but marked by two tragedies: a collision on an icy highway at the end of her first semester that broke her back in two places, and the death at 52 of her mother, whom Schroeder nursed for two months on leave from Cornell. Schroeder served on the editorial staff of *Epoch*, Cornell's professional literary journal, for three years;

assisted and taught in the freshman seminar program for two years; and graduated with a Master of Fine Arts in Creative Writing in 1985, six days after the birth of her daughter, Clara Bosak-Schroeder, now a professor of Classics at the University of Illinois.

In 1986, with a husband and daughter to support and no reliable academic work in prospect, Schroeder moved the family back to Southern California and then to the San Francisco Bay Area, where they lived until she and her husband returned to Ithaca in 2005.

In California, Schroeder worked as an emergency room, intensive care, and cardiac care nurse while attending San Jose State University, where she gained a Master of Science in Community Nursing in 1992. For the next 13 years, she served variously as staff developer, director of organizational development, and director of quality improvement and case management at hospitals and home care agencies in the Bay Area. At the time of her return to Ithaca, she was clinical manager of the largest and oldest hospice in San Francisco. She also served for several years as president of the Bay Area Society for Healthcare Education and Training and a member and chair of the Greater South Bay Regional Home Care Council. For her early involvement with the SGML/XML Special Interest Group of HL7, the organization that sets technical standards for health care informatics, and for her pioneering articles on telemonitoring, she received the Information Technology Award of the nursing honor society Sigma Theta Tau in 1997.

In addition to raising a daughter and providing critical support for her husband's career in the computer industry, Schroeder continued to pursue work as a medical writer, producing, among other publications, standard introductions to home health care and hospice care. She was a regular contributor to *NURSEweek*, *Healthweek*, and *Home Health Focus*, and she served for two years as a member of the editorial review board of the *Journal of the National Association of Vascular Access Nurses* and four years as a member of the editorial review board of *Home Health Focus*. She also continued to teach, as an instructor in undergraduate English programs and graduate-level community health at the University of Phoenix from 1996 through 1999 and as a teacher of writing in the undergraduate Health Professions program at San Jose State University from 1997 to 2005.

Shortly after returning to Ithaca in 2005, intending to spend the rest of her life writing, Schroeder joined the Ithaca Health Alliance to help work on the organization's newsletter. In 2006, she was elected to the IHA's board of directors, and shortly thereafter she was elected board president, a position she held from 2006 to 2010. As president, Schroeder guided the IHA through a complete rechartering in order to resolve a bitter, longstanding dispute with the Internal Revenue Service and gain a critical 501(c)(3) designation as a nonprofit organization. She also negotiated, planned, and personally supervised the relocation of the IHA's Ithaca Free Clinic to the greatly expanded facilities it now occupies. In the summer of 2010 she became the first executive director of the IHA and the Free Clinic, a position she held until her retirement in March 2012. In her time with the IHA, Schroeder wrote or cowrote grant applications and supervised fundraising efforts that brought in over a million dollars to the organization. For her work with the IHA, she received the Tompkins Trust Company Award for Excellence in 2009, a Cornell Civic Leaders Fellowship for 2009–2010, and the Ithaca Neighborhood Housing Services Lucy J. Brown Leadership Award in 2010.

In addition to her work with the IHA, Schroeder was also notable in the local community as a member of the board of directors of Sustainable Tompkins from 2007 to 2009 and a cofounder of TCLocal, an organization dedicated to building local resiliency in the face of energy descent and climate change. Several articles authored by Schroeder on the subject of health care and energy are available on the tclocal.org web site. Her last published article was a piece she cowrote on seed saving that appeared in *The Natural Farmer*, the newspaper of the Northeast Organic Farming Association.

Schroeder died October 22, 2012 after a brief and unexpected illness. She was 60 years old.

Joy Ladin has published ten books of poetry, including her new collection, *Shekhinah Speaks* (Selva Oscura Press); National Jewish Book Award winner *The Book of Anna*; *The Future is Trying to Tell Us Something: New and Selected Poems*; and Lambda Literary Award finalists *Transmigration* and *Impersonation*. She is also the author of a memoir, National Jewish Book Award finalist *Through the Door of Life*, and another work of creative non-fiction, Lambda Literary and

Triangle Award finalist *The Soul of the Stranger*. Her work has been recognized with a National Endowment for the Arts Fellowship, a Fulbright Scholarship, an American Council of Learned Societies Research Fellowship, and a Hadassah Brandeis Institute Research Fellowship, among other honors. Her writing is available at joyladin.wordpress.com.

www.ingramcontent.com/pod-product-compliance
Lightning Source LLC
Chambersburg PA
CBHW040742120726
48007CB00007B/68